Buy a Ticket

Buy a Ticket

New and Selected Poems by Judith R. Robinson

Word Poetry

Published by Word Poetry
P.O. Box 541106
Cincinnati, OH 45254-1106

ISBN: 9781625493996

Poetry Editor: Kevin Walzer
Business Editor: Lori Jareo

Visit us on the web at www.wordpoetrybooks.com

to Pittsburgh:
beautiful, rugged, nurturing city;
my place in the world

Table of Contents

Love Story

What did it take
To make Alex smile?

History, Mystery,
Biscotti, and Fries.

But potatoes, soup, and jazz—
Those translated to love.

When did the tale begin?
Many decades of Saturdays ago.

How did it sound?
Eager and sweet as Fats on the Hill

How did it look?
Dips into blue: rivers, irises, skies.

How did it taste?
Easy to say, just imagine: ripe bananas, very rich cheese.

How did it work?
Hard to say: but imagine Alex: Handsome, Uncertain, Unto Himself.

How did it end?
Cannot say, but imagine: inarticulate grief.

What did I learn?
Nothing. Something. A lot.

Much Can Be Missed

White for stately homes
in London and Charleston.
The flag of surrender.

Pink for dimpled cheeks
and other soft items
that harden then disappear.

Glaucous purple blossoms
wounds of the elderly
that never heal.

Gray the steady march
from presence to absence
the going until gone.

Love is sought in every season;
desperate, the pull of its scarlet patina;
for this much can be missed;

Mauve, ecru, lemon, beige,
the subtle blushes,
washes, blends and hues.

Father's Day Poem

My father smoked Camels, two packs a day.
He wore a fedora, worked like crazy,
and believed he was lucky,
that his life was better than his father's.
They're not as hard on the Jews now—
I heard him tell my Uncle Dave, many times.
Actually, they discussed how good or bad things
were for the Jews for forty years.
And who the enemies were, which
ones were worse than the others,
and the Pirates, the poor Pirates,
always in the cellar, year after year.

Questions

What do I know of hunger?
They say the starving dream of food.
I heard Depression era stories
My mother's painful account: *days with nothing to eat.*
I confused her with Cinderella.

What do I know of hunger?
They say the starving dream of food.
There were childhood commandments
My father's admonition: *please finish everything on the plate.*
There were children in Europe with nothing.

What do I know of hunger?
In dreams I see old lovers, old cities,
I fall from trees and mountains,
Forget exams, speeches, names of others.
They say the starving dream of food.

What is the difference between hunger
And starvation?
A few days, a week or so?
A difference in dreams, perhaps?

April

They weep,
the sweet unsprung buds.
They cringe
and hide, perilously
bent beneath
skies restless and dark
as widow's weeds
as rivers rise
in western Pennsylvania.
Does this gloom
portend a raging death
or will it yield to
something tender?
Shall we weep with them
or wait? When I was young
and clear and wise
I knew the answer:
Hold fast, I'd say, tomorrow
comes in green and gold
and you and I will lust
and live forever.

Mary Lou, *Last Summer*

heat rules   burns everything
green curls to rust

sun presses down
a simpering smile-button

the dejected landscape
consorts with her bitterness

at night Banjo Ted
a little wine   soiled linens

hours pass somehow until
the heavy breath he exhales

raises sweetish bile
chokes her throat

midnight desperation   she runs
he tries   but does not catch her

hammering away on   the club's
the gym's   the ship's   locked doors

the song he writes   *Last Summer*
weaves the story his way

heroism his twangy
theme   a simple three chord strum

Like Levana, Jewess of Cordoba

Soul, abide
with me.
Move lightly
in the easy way
of children.

The earth
is home for now.
Let me sway to the rhythm
of festival harps.

I polish my skin
with precious oils,
adorn my neck
with colored stones,
rubies that blaze, the greenest emeralds;
press my lips to pages
of sacred text.

Tonight I lap up the world like wine,
and do not foresee an empty glass.

Saturday, Buenos Aires, Following the Coup

The bare walls dazzle—
antiseptic white and cold.
Curious, so little left
but bayonets stacked & gleaming
in the corner like bones
fresh-stripped of skin,
spotless as the whole room.
Not a drop of blood anywhere.

The Maestro
licks his fat lips,
raises his baton.
At once the restless crowd,
the beautiful portenos, is stilled.
Alvaro and the woman begin
the tango, the evening specialty.

He dips deep forward,
her hair brushes the floor.
Her smooth leg
arches high and tenses,
intersecting his back.

The music stops,
the portenos, caught, stare,
echo the silence.

Then only motion and the dancer's
flat, locked-together eyes,
quick silhouettes flashing
across the polished floor.

At the end, well-paid,
Alvaro and the woman bow
to the hushed musicians,
and back away, past the vivid crowd,
into the sparkling night
of palms and vacant streets.

Counting

When I imagine time
or my age or almost any amount
of anything I see numbers on
blue-lined-grainy first-grade paper,

penciled columns in tens
from one to seventy-nine on the front,
the eighties, nineties, and the very
important one hundred on the back.

They say we make these cerebral connections.

So here you are with me, again, more than
three-quarters of the way across the front page.
There are still small chippy flecks in the cheap
paper, just as before, when we were still
far over on the left side of the page.

Well, every column
that came in between has passed, all of it,
our lives in common, and not,
so much and so little embedded in those wavy columns!

Soon, my love, still counting,
we must face the matter of turning the page.

What She Does for Melvin

In this accidental universe,
Mevin tries to describe the stars.

Their silver points assault his eyes,
stun him through the prism of his tears.

Melvin envies slinky women,
the glamour of old movies,

night-walking strangers in dark raincoats,
famous tragedians, slap-happy clowns.

He finds and tries the steepest trails,
twists along their winding furrows,

a fool of a human chasing dreams
down a lowroad called Confusion.

A silhouette beneath the trees:
a kindred someone hiding

bears witness, bargains, even begs
comfort for him from the drifting yellow moon.

Wishing for Carson Street
for Weldon Kees and Woody Allen, after reading Poecology Magazine

Night in a country field
hissing bugs, the sky
pockmarked with stars
ugly bright spilled beans
that glare and sting
and oppress my eyes.

Makes me wish
for curbs and city lights
cement and storefronts
men with tattooed bodies
and strutting girls
their boozy songs
their dirty streets
their blah blah blah.

A Dream of My Cousin

My cousin Dora, born before me,
had been loved; grew up
invincible as anyone at sixteen,

when onto her unsuspecting head
a nightmare of night descended.

Every day became fetid night
of *Sophia the Gentile* no longer Dora
Dora gone Dora no longer alive.

The blur became walls splintered
from fire and   grain fields high enough
and caverns deep enough   anywhere anywhere
to hide to move   to never stay long

run run run

never sleep long   eat   anything anything
green in the dirt keep moving   keep breathing
another bridge another barn

run run run

until on the last of all nights
she lay spent   a gray silhouette
sunk to the ground
of a musky forest.

Something small scuttered by.

Dora again, in the end,
crawling after it,
whispering, crooning, pleading
to touch its softness.

Brief Bio

I: born into freedom
few limits inflicted
parental craziness:
my father, a stone, silent;
my mother, a secret gambler,
consequently a liar;
I, her quick-tongued accomplice.

I: a wild green weed, a pest
growing thick hellbent limbs
driving my wheels through the muck
craving sugar, ballet shoes,
other kids, the boy next door.

I: growing up, harboring secrets,
wishing for love
bossing my little brother around.
Nobody beat me up.

I: only one young promise kept
to escape the mob never be part of it
the prize, a critical mind a knowing.

I: remaindered: the need to plod on
the bind: these guts and this soul
all my sweet dead   all the wanting.

June

The well
at the base of the throat
the small hollow
where certainty once dwelt
is now the hiding place for tears.

My best pal had verve—
he had more young adventures
than disappointments—
more even than
the every hair counted
on his fearless crown.

Once we kibitzed around
our magic places—
laughed so much of the time
because with quick fingers
he could launch fat red balloons
of silliness wrapped
in slyness that would drown me
in the universe of the slaphappy
whenever he wanted.

June is the cruelest month for me.
The long, sunlit, grievous days
of June.

Buy a Ticket

An old, diminished town.
Broken streets, broken glass.
Walls here are layered
Many coats of paint, all peeling.
Flakes of rust glom on to any metal.
The salt does this.

A lone surprise amidst the grit:
A chrome-bright gym open
Twenty-four-seven for the afflicted
The jobless-wounded-welfare-ians who
Nagging at scabs, cannot sleep.

Someone says dance, someone says hope,
Someone says Wal Mart is coming;
Someone says try this, it will take off the edge
No one on the other side knows squat but

Of one truth the pounded-bruised-lacerated
Are certain—money would make everyone happy.

A Visitor

A visitor enters my space
an impervious spirit
with a face
stiff as clay.
Her name is *Gefuhllosigkeit*
which means *Numbness.*
She sits and stares
with cold blind eyes.

I wish she would leave.

Adorno calls her *Noya.*
Ennui, his way.
He knows her as I do
but he wastes no wishes.
He knows where she came from.

Says she rode in on a backwash,
pale filthy water in the wake
of the ship that carried off
the garden nymphs the Jewbirds
the ancestors whose names I knew.

She makes prey of me and prevails.

Adorno has better weapons,
his ferocious will
his less perturbed heart.
Unlike me
he will never
let her outdo him.

We Will Dance the Hootchie-Cootchie
for my grandmother, Dora Silverman Ruttenberg

I am a child, yet she is almost my size.
I never put this into words, or even thoughts
But I feel it; we are both small.
Her hands, however, are wide and worn down,
Adult hands, old even, netted with thick blue veins
She lets me press and feel as we sit together
In the swing on the porch. I say this is fun
And she laughs and sings with me, always the same song:
Meet Me in St. Louie, Louie, Meet Me at the Fair...
There is no one else to see us rocking and singing
About dancing the Hootchie-Cootchie. She doesn't
Care that I don't sing well or my legs are too short
To be a ballerina. My drawings line her walls.
She calls me *mine kint*. She thinks I will be an artist.

Birdland
for *Father Patrick Desbois*

A lamentation of swans
their sleek necks bared
without the mercy of water;

Jewels now found under fields
of Ukrainian weeds and wildflowers,
the grassy slopes of Rawa-Ruska, Belarus;

This was the rude east,
The fields different than the west;
Vast, vivid and green, no boxcars rolling.

The sacrifice:
one precious metal slug per Jewbird.
Each well-aimed, well-spent.

Numbers newly unearthed
Your kleine bubba, and mine.
Each a ghastly postscript to history.

Picnic at Belarus
another for Father Patrick Desbois

1.

The children are there, too.
Some know the Mozart,
Others are bored.

Late afternoon: they march around.
Imitate the soldiers.
The parents lay out the picnic.
The wursts and cabbage. The clamor for sweets.

2.

This was the verdant east,
murder fields different than the west;
The children accept it,
Keep their thoughts to themselves.
Rat-a-tat! Rat-a-tat!
They fall down brilliantly.

3.

Costly: one vital metal bullet per Jew.
Newly found, an addendum to the story.
Torn hankies wipe the milky mouths;
The real hand waves goodbye again.

early on

when the pale March sun
overtakes the remains of old snow
there's the gray slush of childhood again
the slogging through it
up Barnsdale hill
for lunch at home;

I see baby Kathie,
eat a good chicken pot pie
heated up by Maybelle
watch Joanne Barron kiss Arthur Tate
on her *Search for Tomorrow.*

and oh! that other deliciousness:
the taste of life to come.

Proud Violet

Today
a broad-beamed woman
at the bus stop,
perspiring

in her flowered hat
flowered dress
flowered hanky

standing alone
in the cloudlight

all dressed up
for Sunday.

I recognize her,
a solitary spray
of violet
petals glistening
in the downtown dust.

The wrong bus
lumbers by
trailing a blast of heat;
she leans back, stiffens,
and at once I yearn

to touch her
say I'm sorry
for the empty road
the long-gone friends
the absent children,

those kids who fled
these gray steel hills,
these sunless, broken streets.

The sky darkens,
an odd, metallic amber.
I nod to her from the window.
She blinks, turns,
lifts her wilted head,
and gazes past me.

Why I Love My Lipstick

Because, in Clearly Crimson, I can sing a siren's song.
Because, in Crystal Coral, I am never alone too long.

I can name the stars for Martin, wearing Starlit Pink.
Or speak my mind to Phillip, tell him what I think.

Because, in Lilac Rose, I do not hide in bed;
I can out-dazzle anybody, wearing All Star Red.

Because, in Silvery Mauve, I lay claim to copper skies;
Because in Copperglaze Brown, I never apologize.

At night, by Naked Bronze Glow, I hear my lover sing
Inside his purple kisses, I drink Wine With Everything.

In the August of my life I still savor Cherries In The Snow
And treasure the girlish heart that compels me to do so.

I am Boldness, Beauty, Devil & Charmer
In a beeswax, coal tar & fragrance armor.

Somewhere

Somewhere a chestnut horse plods
along a leafy trail.
His steady rider also nods.
They move as one, one bent
unit rolling like a song
up and down the shifting rays.

Off to find another place, they hum, easy as summer.

It may seem they've left me here,
amid the noise and street-scapes,
but in the airborne scatter of the song
I am riding with them.

When we get there, there are apple trees
golden as late September, shedding for us,
the horse, the rider and for me.

The juice is warm but slakes our thirst.
The drenching sun slides to four o'clock.
Quick with joy and sweat we three mount up
and find the trail again.

A Good Cry, and Spirits are Served

Irony hides behind the dancing skirts
of Humor, her pink-cheeked, ample mother.

Clever daughter, she waits until
Mother stops for breath, then sneaks around to chase
Limerick, her naughty cousin. Limerick, that ribald fool,
chuckles even as she passes him up, overtakes him
to arrive first at the door of Satire's elegant soiree.

She slips easily past Rap, the agile bouncer...

Woah! All the Swell Elements are there, amid the witty furnishings:
Conceit, supine on the long white couch, dripping diamonds.
Hard to detect in pale gray silk are Ambiguity, swaying in the corner
with Ambivalence, neither sure of where to sit...

At the moonlit window, Haiku rests upon tiny brush-painted pillows.
Villanelle takes turns with Rondo, boldly running up
then tumbling down the stairs. Free Verse sprawls all over the floor,
discarding peanut shells and fruit peels where he will,

to the annoyance of Ode, Sonnet, and Sestina, who stiffen with
disapproval.
They, and all assembled, are awaiting the synchronized
arrival of the evening's entertainers, Madrigal and Lyric...

The beautiful pair, so terribly old now, but so eternally passionate.

At last, these two sweep into the room. A hush descends
as Lyric takes up his instrument, Madrigal clears her throat.
The evening has deepened, blue to purple; the audience settles in.
Lyric plucks the lyre: sweet, sad melodies pour forth.

Madrigal lifts her silvery voice and sings, most achingly,
of death's immutable claim on all lovers.
Moans and sighs punctuate the silence that follows.

Most subtly, Irony turns away her head, lest the others see
that even she has shed a tear.

The Burning Yearn

to be the singular self
not another identical
clam shell or duck that walks, talks,
and is a duck, no hardworking worker ant,
sly city mouse, or other pretty face;
not a cow in a herd nor a drop in an ocean trough:
Bonnie Lynn Meltzer,
holy, whole, single, separate, insistent,
gazing at the blooming moon
with unpuzzled eyes
guarding memories
of other summer moons,
10 k races won
fireflies and a porch swing
brother Dan and cousin Ann,
Teddy next door yet so far away,
Uncle Hal, in from Buffalo,
his big bald sweating head
his happiness cooling off
in the family plastic pool,
those many summers ago.

everyone

I tell everyone to try
to take note of things
that are improvements
like soft foaming soap in a bottle
vastly sturdier tires
air in the shrunken city—
so much cleaner that men don't
wash cars on Saturdays anymore;
everyone is wearing black
and talking on small personal phones
many are fat and no one smokes
but everyone knows the way
to stay alive is movement
dance spin run yoga make room
for those bikes but watch out—
everyone runs the red lights.

Collateral Circulation

Can a badly-worn oak receive
a graft of fresh branch
that actually works well?

When both its inbound
and outbound paths are blocked
the heart is still served.

Tunnels that route blood
expand into brand new byways
circumvent old grief-laden scar tissue;

they are smaller, they pinch their way
around all the fat and flaw,
serve to keep the animal running.

So much for metaphor.
Please understand that the heart does not quite break.
Neither is it ever quite repaired.

It shrinks to semblance.

Feed Lots

My head is clamorous with morning.
Before me crowds are trampling the pathways.
Up for breakfast, they rush
to feed at counters & tables;

True, at night they lust to dance,
to play, to curl beneath
bedcovers; by day, to decorate
and embrace themselves.

True, some will remember
a moment of trout shared at
a windswept lake in summer,
a kindly word, a promise.

If once happy, feeding, they will nod,
smile, and choose a rounded spoon.
If starved, take care: they will
find the sharpest knife.

The Pure Sky World to Come

I see the raw land
from the hold of a filthy scow.

The shore has darkened from gold to rust,
The plovers and the gulls gone missing.

The sheltered path has become
a twisted road, bowers beaten away.

My lips form an open O.
My voice a squall the wind bears forth:

Is there still virgin ground?   a stone a stalk
a place firm enough to stack

this wild grief
that swallows down so hard splits

bone raw   crusts flesh
at the tender core
the spot where Hope once sat

pure dumb Hope poured
her incandescent light
like a child spills milk

God if you can hear
it hurts to stay
where every path falls dead away

& my heart's worn sore
this may be about
much too much
and not a moment more

this may be want,
this may be need
of the pure sky world to come.

This Pittsburgh Moment, 2015
for Donald Featherstone

Saint James Street
At mid-afternoon.
The sound of traffic.
Wheeling, humming.

A window box
Of orange roses
Outer petals gone pale
In full sunlight.

Down on Fifth
Dangerous numbers
Staggering toe to toe
Bumper to bumper
Along the broken street.

They must work
To collect the fat
To stake the flag
Up the golden pole.
To drag every living thing
From the swift gray river.

The Chinese doctor
Who never speaks
Pulls into the spotty shade
Of his driveway.

CNN reports the father
Of the pink flamingo
Has died.

No more white ice cream
Trucks, very few honey bees.
No more starlit hay rides
Or other glowing events.

Attention Amazon: Pittsburgh

What land is this, what city?
Aren't other places as precious to those
who dwell within them?
Probably they are. Well, perhaps.

But here instead of sunshine there are gray skies,
gloom as delicious as heavy dark beer.
Green hills that slope into swift deep rivers,
moving their own way, no one else's.
Old trees all over town, in the parks, lining city sidewalks,
along the broken alleys.

Neighborhoods of stone mansions.
Neighborhoods of clean aluminum-sided and red-brick houses.
Porches with swings, blooming gardens.

Grand old families, lying dead in leafy cemeteries,
near libraries and museums and universities bearing their names.
Tough old ethnic families, lying dead in leafy cemeteries,
near riverbanks where mills rose up to manufacture
the steel for trains and autos that opened up the country;
wheels and planes and tanks and weapons
that saved the world again and again.

And we the living descendents, the incredible mix of all here before us,
the boys and girls of the adversaries turned friends: Wasps and Hunkies,
the Blacks and the Jews, the Italians and Asians, we are the heirs
to the first river traders and fur hunters, the freed slaves,
the immigrant industrial barons and immigrant mill hands.

And that sometimes adversarial past.
The burning truth of *Out Of This Furnace*.
The '36 confrontation at Republican Steel.
The birth agony of big steel and big labor.
And since, the death agony, too.

Okay. A grand old city (old for America, that is)
with an interesting past, wonderful people, a lousy climate (some think).
So why the heart pull, looking at the hills? Hills, you might say, are hills.

But we who live here know something. Pittsburgh's been good to us.
We forgive. We co-exist. We get along.

gloss and chaos

the fire drills the glue the iron gray stairwells
the mimeographs of poems smeared blue with tears
you and i hiding in the back of class aware
of what terror could occur right there with a pointer
or downtown with the pumped-up weekend marchers
the rag-tag adults we wanted so to be
but came to see as ruthless in their grasp
hobbled by the hammers of their conceit

now alive in a season of full captivity
thursdays noted for fat newspapers
fatter with extra sections that will
never address the iceblock cold
nerves stretched tight as wire
so much effort to hold bitterness at bay
in the silence that crushes any thought
that a song we loved might still somehow matter

A Brother Writes His Blessings

Martin, a contemplative Jew,
follows the example of Elijah
into a cave of solitude
far from the hustle and bustle
of existence to hear
the still small voice:

Just me and peace
no other faces;
no sweat on palms
no winking eyes;
deep release from lies: just me.

He has turned from the earthquake,
the wind, and the city;
they have too long obscured
the call to slip to a deeper level:

Just me and prayer:
a book of pages
to turn like leaves;
holy the tree whose core
has turned to pages.

He will live
in this dusky place
without distraction
from voices of humans
or chirping of birds.

No sound no praise
no nether days;
just this place
this summer cave
to savor.

At once bonded
and flung free
he will stay to chant,
to sway, to feast on psalms
and sweet conundrums.

Now the sadness

of searching for one lost
and not found in memory but
for a static camera image:

the same twist of body
dodging the swells
a smile at fourteen
reflecting bright sunlight
a striped bathing suit
the bluegreen Atlantic;

what perverse circuitry
of suffering brain fastens on this
utter stillness, this image caught
forever in an unmovable moment

sans touch, sans smell, sans taste;
why only the eye, the eye
as lordly registrar of what was,
why the partnership with torment

that hoards a berry scent,
a young baritone,
a mother's kiss on tender skin…
why this outrage, this thievery?

If this was a movie

I would drift back
onto a slope in Pittsburgh
when my ballerina days
were still a dream
and the kids on the block
found what to do
that had nothing to do
with parents.

Only the bike named Betsy
negotiated for me,
helping me always win
down the hill, the street hill
not the cemetery hill.

All before I cared about any other wanting.

No big questions.
We may as well have been
tomatoes or anything else
alive that grows regardless,
like tomatoes.
What mattered was the bike
—racing—more than jacks
more than tar-baby stop
much more than Monopoly.

If there was thought
it was not deep
or has been forgotten,
slipped back, flickering,

a blurry frame
silver-gray as were those skies
if
this
was
a movie.

Carousel

I who want speed
    tumble
        & crash

struggle to right myself

ponies bow down
ivory teeth bared
nostrils spread wide

I roll to my left
    creep
        to my knees

ponies spin on
edges blend & blur
angels & cherubs watch

        my body go down
           again
          & again

ponies rear back
painted hoofs rise
blank eyes stare

        full circle mechanics
           fuel whistles & horns
               plexiglass hearts

wounds will heal
swellings recede
scars will be pink

      but not pretty
        unlikely roses
          roses as bruises
              on limbs & on lips

& ponies spin on

Besotted

*Listen: When it rains it rains
all over the world!*

a child's cherished idea: perfect
to engage another battle
with the cretins smirking on the corner.
Kamika gulps down trouble;
swallows each laugh,
feels a bloodscar settle
underneath her smooth bronze
surface, her magic exterior:
the umber that masks
foolishness, secrets and shame,
damage that has no cure.

Yet so madly in love
with sweeping pronouncements
so besotted with ideas
that might turn tides
she will never stop
the chorus, the forays,
the enchantment;
not then, not now, not ever.

After Words

When this curious world wearies
of me, and me of it, if an eerie tunnel

aflow with muck & a filthy scow
happens to beckon me

though chill-edged and pounding with fear
I will recognize it & I may go for it,

get on board as engines groan in reverse,
sail back through the blackness—

for I would gladly leave here & now to eat lunch
with my father at Marky's in the Strip,

& I want to take another crack at big
blond Mary Gordan even though

I know she will wield after everyone
with her fat arms and evil hockey stick;

I want the greasy delicious egg rolls
from Kelly Street on Friday night

& to look up at giants who smoke two packs a day
& never lock their doors & never leave me.

We all sit in the Roadmaster, watch the burning hills
the sky lit red with fire & then we are riding home.

Time is weird, suspended;
there's no boat back & I don't care—

a June dusk deepens from purple blue to
starlit as the roof opens, the operetta begins:

I keep my eyes open. I listen. Quixote sings his dream,
strings quiver, they weep, and I stay put.

Art Deco

The hotel is vast and pink
squatting on a southern shore
grand old palm trees
turquoise water
shimmering waves of white heat.

I am running the burnished halls
that reek money
I am not naked
exactly but searching for my nightie.
Butlers in tuxedos are on the lookout.

I can't get the elevator
to come for me
can't remember which room I had;
utterly lost and out of ideas.

But I don't cry, don't give up,
just keep dashing around
in full frenzy,
the angry butlers closing in on me.

They don't get me. I wake up.
Just in time to tell
the whole wretched tale to Y.

She listens, nods in her wise way
then goes to the kitchen to make coffee.
The paper says rain she says
and you're not too old to dream.

Ah, Faith!

Orphee's agony coincides
in mystery   in irony   in truth
with the Satmar and Lubovitch—
breathless Jews in black frock coats
twisting through the hot-baked
streets of Crown Heights,
their wives running behind
dripping sweat under fashion wigs—
pulling gaggles of kinder
past the Kundalini Yogis of Soho
whose gleaming eyes flicker
whose breath comes
in deep gasps of ecstasy
rocking chanting davening swaying
all of them rooted to the earth
like ancient conifers
certain as rain in spring
that every human hair is counted
every snowflake a blessed original
as the glorious universe spins on
palpably innocent   athrob   unfolding
exactly as it is meant to.

A Climate for Children

Clouds, shaded soft
as dove's wings,
yield most days
to showers, sometimes sweet,
but often harsh
as the first days of mourning,

as when spring
rains moisture
upon the cold earth,
heaps wetness
on us all, lies heavy
in the chilled trees,

as well as on the children;

mists them
green-barked and thick-skinned
forcing growth along sloping streets,
streets of bricks and poles and wires
without the steady
sun of other places;

perhaps this is why
the hardy sprouts never hide
from unsparing light:
they learn early to stretch,
to climb, to bob high,
to forgive and love each other.

Desperados

1.
At first, when a lack of rain came upon us
we paid scant attention.
We had just met Tom and fair Ann.
We meant to water the garden more often;
mentioned it, twice, on the Fourth of July.

2.
Summer wore on. For want of water
the wrens flew away.
You decided to go to the Cape,
a shipwright's job might be available.
The garden had drifted dry as ash,
the vines withered to brown.
We had let it all go.

3.
I wore a party dress, lavender and gold,
when we met, accidentally,
next year in September.
You reminded me of Barret Welles,
the copyist of Renoir
who rendered dresses like mine
in bold blots of color.

4.
Our lovemaking that afternoon
happened with purpose, with weight;
we held on as true as we could,
as if there were still chances:
one more grand summer storm,
green lightening,
a murderous downpour of rain.

An Adventure

H. saw a rat
In the back
Of Rosenbloom's Bakery
Where she worked
The summer she was fifteen.
It was gray and huge
And the first of its kind
She ever met.
Naturally she screamed
And dropped a tray
Of fresh baked kichel.
Also working at the bakery
Was an extremely old countess
Way down on her luck
Here in America.
Among the family stories
We tell we mention
This as the summer
Of the rat and the countess.
An adventure from
The bright green time
Of becoming for H.
Which certainly
Seemed a beginning
But like all starts
Are often false and lead
Down ways that
Smoothly rise
And unexpectedly fall
But always end.

Spring Fever

The desire in the old man's mind
is a stone anchor
that keeps his boney feet tethered
to the home place, dirt and all:

to own the first intruding green
he sees, the almost gold
that should burst to green
during his daily watch.

He must not miss the moment,
fears it may come forth
at once, like sudden water:
pouring, seamless.

His craving appears each spring.
He suspects this must be by design,
simple and meant to be, the way
morning overtakes the brightest moon.

Otherwise he would be able;

unpossessed, he would turn away,
free to leave the garden.

Tikkun Olam*

Woven with care
Red silk ribbon
Shot through with gold
To shimmer in starlight—

The soft fabric spoke
Of being ripped,
Her threads pulled apart
Her heart frayed
Into trailings no
Gentlewoman's needle
Could ever repair—

Yet each of them
Tried, wielding silver
Tools, stretching slender
Fingers, gathering, pricking—
Yet never nimble enough
To knit the tears,
To stop the bloody flood—

Strong but not enough
To let it be, to walk away.

* *Hebrew for Repair the World*

Spring Light in the City

She feels
a heaviness
on her chest
burdensome as
the memory
of woolen layers
forced on her
by Mother
even as the sun
melted crystalline
snowy days
into seepage
down the slopes
so long ago;
curious how
pale spring light
in afternoon
bears back
that weight,
that gloom,
unchanged.

Blessed

In my mind's eye

the outline
of my own warm kidney

its vital kidney shape,

blessed above my waist,
filtering, functioning,
behaving, a work of innards
without me, but for me,

set there with grace.

Other organic whys…
a man who is a woman
inside and knows it

begs, borrows, steals
his mother's purse
to get the operation;

Melvin in holy torment
sacrifices blood & body

to be Mandy.

They weep within me now.
I wrap my arms around us
and rock awhile,

soothing over mysteries.

Dilemma

As children
Our willing hearts
Encompass them.
The little lamb frolics
Across Little Golden pages
So do the tiny piglets.
We learn to say baa, baa,
Oink, oink, oink
And smile.
But behind our lips
Our own baby teeth come in
And fall out like wisdom;
Then we grow canines
And it is constantly time to eat.

urbanity

how to tolerate crowds
of human strangers
all those bodies that sweat
and push and displace
space and air and seats
on buses or clog the roadways
I don't mean robbers
rapists or molesters
or anything like that
I mean the strangers who
load up on wine in restaurants
and scream their shrill
heads off when you are trying to eat
the ones who smell lousy
that you have to wait behind
in long lines at the store
the ones who run red lights
and cut you off in traffic
and what about all the pretending
that goes on? One honest curmudgeon
said hell is other people but few
will admit that is the truth
nor will most admit a reasonable
preference for dogs.

Come March

amidst
the last snowflakes
a warbler calls

pushing
through hard dark earth:
daffodils

near the
freezing window
robin's nest

blowing
over fists of buds:
an easy wind

through
puddles of rain and mud
the worm renews

beyond
our wounds and fictions:
another spring

A Gift

An old scene wafts in
on fumes of mill sulphur:

thin November sunlight breaks
through scudding clouds

above our swaddled heads, and we move slowly,
over-bundled like babies, but that is our lot:

our anxious mother, a flapping hen;
our hardworking father, always silent.

our warm child's breath mingles,
we puff at each other

and on the ice drops suspended
from twigs, caught mid-freeze;

then we set to digging down in the new snow,
sweating in cold joy, determination,

our whole hearts in the work.

We will measure the snowfall,
create great white piles,

and find the real bottom of things.

Larry is stronger, but I am older, smarter.
He listens to me, lets me direct.

This is how it happened when we were small.

Now a wisp of late afternoon
skylight rushes me back,

and in a magic snatch of time
before the fade, we are together again.

Genius

Breathing short and frowning
victim and survivor
you hint at sins
dark as clotted blood
secrets lurid as tabloid lies.
You cannot describe
the blows that fell upon you but:
this is why
I am as I am
you say with soft wet eyes
weeping within words
dying a little
with every reminiscence,
but beautiful to me;
like rare white sparrows
flying through cloud-light
your brilliant hands
stretch upward
working hard to sculpt
a finer truth,
choosing to go on.

What Joy There Was

Young or old, skin serves:
borders keep innards in place.
Young or old, we believe wings
encompass universal detritus:
car keys, single socks, diamonds,
Erno's cracked limbs,
his woman's fat hips,
her mother's sagging knees,
the dogwood's budding branches.
We believe all is counted.
Yet Erno's gang is not much involved—
it goes on with or without them.
The waters ripple and flow with fish
and even if reproduction slows in Europe,
it does not halt. Therefore
the gang chooses hard
to remember what joy there was
in Miami, the Christmas of 98,
they watched, with their little boy,
the plastic pine tree change
from bright red to white to cobalt blue
then, at once, to all the glory colors.

Lazlo's Trip

Water holds no conviction,
the hills, no guilt.

Eyes like ours water
innocent and mauve with tears

even as bloated fish
ripple through waves

bearing off the crumbs
of heavy sin.

Lazlo traveled to Key West
and found a day cruise

for gay men only, lonely ones
only, no couples allowed.

He cruised and was happy,
buoyant, until clouds

purpled with rain and overtook
the stinging sun.

The men despaired
the snorkeling was ruined

despite what other small
joys remained for them.

Some storytellers believe
answers can be supplied,

and mysteries solved.
Some, like Lazlo, think not.

Modne Teg, Modne Nacht*

The young abandon day for dreamy night
eager beneath the yellow moon
rolling with simple pleasure.

Wrapped in moments of flesh
they seem to soar above the lion and the lamb.
They glimpse beyond the blowing stars.

They believe in the gorgeous present.

Do they know that other days will follow?
Strange days. Strange nights.
Moons will grow dim and blacken.
Seas will yearn and rise.

Suns will bear down, over-heating land,
bleaching away what grows,
disrupting the ordered song.

Unease will creep in, then blanket.

After fits of nervy eruption,
hemming and speculation,
there will be no more cries to you,
no further trust that you will hear.

The one left waiting to disappear
by morning will find confusion
in the tight green buds,
oddness in the celebration.

Hebrew for Strange Days, Strange Nights

Knowings

There are knowings
You deny me:
the wisdom of
a gentle cow,
the purple cowslip,
a graceful dove.
The certainty
of a storm,
the busy sycamore,
its sap,
its falling bark.

What I do
is plant tomatoes,
will them
to redden, believing
they are mine.
Here, in this field
where willows
wave against
a silent sky,
I am all my
yearnings,
foolish
in ways which
they are not.

Gone, Good-bye, Encore

I am one who knows what
parting is,
the drawn and quartered
feel of it, the near-fatal tearing.

The word good-bye,
the word gone, are its
smallest prongs,
slivers of glass
working their sharp ways through
the flesh.

We loved each other once,
before the wounding.
Then Time,
that voracious beast
galloped by
devouring everything,
everything good
everything rotten.

Still yesterday
by chance
we stood in a line
next to one another.
You nodded
your own nod,
half-sweet, half-public,
then off you went, and there they
were again, drawing blood again,

those jagged word-spikes,
those tiny stinging blades:
Gone. Good-bye.

April 25, 2019

The first true pastel day,
Pink—lime—yellow
made-up so gaudy
the eye tears.
Springtime, late this year.
Three days until my son's birthday,
the only perfect
decision I ever made
in this life. No abortion, so I thank myself.
Forty-six times now.
I pass a workman in a slicker and cap,
wires on the ground around him:
Watch your step!
I will!
And I know learned folk
who say this contretemps matters
as much as my precious son's birth:
every hair on David's head is counted.
So, the workman in the street.
His appearance in the consummate tapestry.

Pink Lady

I reach back
because
you were there
part of the real
swing dancing
the innocent
erotic
sweet-knowing
never-doubting
worth-saving
world.
How is it I hear
the music
so clearly
when it was
so abundantly
yours?

Mama, my lipstick is red
my hair is upswept
my favorite shoes
have platforms
when I slide
into the role
of ghost, the delicious
game in which
your time becomes mine
and I can indulge
the parts of me
that long after
the dazzling
parts of you.

What could be better?
To smell like gardenias
wear low-cut black dresses
sip many cocktails,
smoke many Camels;
To never consider
that Martin or Phillip
might wish
more of us than
a kiss and a dance,
a Pink Lady romance;
Mama, we wet our lips
smooth our seams
bat our eyes
live our dreams
with so many men
we dance
the gilded time away

knowing:
how wonderful
to be woman
what glamour tints
the nights,
what splendor gilds
the days....!

Oh, Mother, I wonder
why must we
ever wake;
You, laughing woman,
the pinkest lady;
I, your chameleon child,
dancing in the shadows.

Heaven

I hope to kiss both my grandmothers,
who I have missed all my life,
to have them cradle & comfort me,
as curled in their arms
and no longer numb, I cry.

I cry as I am rocked back & forth
and passed between them;
my grandmothers' hands stroke my skin
until the ravages of life
that have marked me,
float away & I am pink & tender
& new as first wildflowers.

Then my grandmothers croon
the truth, a cadence sweet & simple,
and at once the onionskin layers
of mind-papering are peeled away
and the confusion that reigned
shoots high & away & scatters,
buck-shot confetti swirling in bright blue air.

And then, unscarred & clean, I understand.
I know why one soul was born—*lean & blessed,*
supple & strong: Joe DiMaggio—!
& sent to this earth on the exact same day
as Jimmy Jones, who came
to our door each June, blind and nodding
in unmatched plaids,
arrived to tune the old player piano.

Everything is explained: my grandmothers
tenderly place each note of precious truth
in a hollowed green melon, carved into a basket
I can carry, and we are blown home, completely;
and all is just as it should be
and never, until this moment, was.

Rage

in remembrance of the Sharpeville Massacre

It disturbs, this slanting light
yellow & rapturous
and once a part of promise.

Mocking now, and strange
these sighing palms
that stirred with expectation.

How like betrayal
the stillness of summer flowers
quiet, beautiful, unfaded.

I was not an alien here.
I was as one with the light
the palms, the lilies.

Why did the earth I loved
not cry out for me
as my life's blood
was sought and taken?

Song for the End of Lithuanian Jewry

Not a charm of goldfinches swirling away
not a clamour of crows in warning
not the sad voice of Kovner,
labeled the fool, urging escape
could penetrate the rays of sunset
striking the leaded glass windows
or find place upon the snowy linens,
or among the crystal wine cups
or golden candles glowing
on the Sabbath table.
No dire word dare enter the quiet after prayers,
the men somber, hushed, still rocking
with praise for the Almighty, and then
the women's dance, their swaying steps,
their rosy children, their clean, kosher homes.
Tonight only the cello is crying.

1945 Song

Drifting, fitful, without sleep, something
looms: a grand gazebo, that once held

vines and blossoms, has splintered and burned,
but I acknowledge a remembered guest,

a slender woman left behind,
rising from the wastes of ash, in bright

pleats of internment cloth, stitched
to shimmer in the almost world.

Head nodding, quietly my mother comes.
She comes from deep unwanted pools

of memory, where other bodies suffered alongside
her own, on a poisoned earth. She touches my arm

and whispers: listen to the warbler
settled in above you; he sounds three notes-

two short, one long and drawn in mercy,
try to hear: for-give-ness!

so sweet his sound, his message!
so sweet, so sweet, so brief!

Turn your cheek, but do not turn away.
Let the notes invade your heart:

only then will you feast on what is left
of dreams, and idle easy in the coming silence.

She pleads for what I cannot give: forgiveness.

Bitter Rain

This day could surely
use some wetting down.
The rain gods are trying; they should.

Dank as Hell on Devonshire,
red oaks made over, a black labyrinth
netting the old mansions.
They are trying hard to make rain; they should.

This day a Polish lady,
tiny, dagger-eyed, shrill,
remembered her long-
past youth when she threw
rock-filled snowballs
at wounded German prisoners
on parade at last
in frozen, rubbled Cracow.

As the iron clouds burst,
reporting how the Krauts bled,
what she screamed:

This is for my father!
This is for my sister!
This is for my Warsaw!

Rain comes. Nothing washes away.

Wakeful

Forgive her: she is afraid to be
near the spot of brain that bled so;
scared to feel the scab let go,
open up, pour forth, to see
the pool, a bloody flood, again, said she.

Bear up! Bear up! she heard the doctor say.
But half-blunderer, she would hide away,
half-coward, reluctant to know
the feel of risky edges.

She fears the Oberhaupt of Thieves,
the crimson tapestry he weaves
the night terror that he dredges.

Deep sleep might offer sweet release,
But what he comes and steals is peace.

Israel Iwler and His Peaceful Cow

After seven hundred
days of night
he emerged,
a stunned Jewbird
on bleeding
hands and knees,
light-blinded by
the years in his
deep cave home.

He came into
the presence of
the green-sprung
world again,
and remembered:

a sun, a moon,
the roof of stars.

It was when
he saw his own
cow, dumb, peaceful,
and not frightened
in the quiet field,
that he fell down

and howled;
savage
beneath a drift of
wind and heedless blossoms
he clawed
and wept
and tore apart
the abundant ground.

Eli, Eli

eleven tolling
orchestral bells
as Elgar tries
with eloquence
to grieve like a Jew
but the cello cries out
O God not again
as I do each New Year
for Akiva for Masada
for the executed
piled deep in pits
at Belarus and Rawa Ruska
for Chelm, Lelow, for Telz,
for the hundreds of shtetls
for Sobibor for Belzec
for the dozens of camps
my people incinerated ghosts
ash in the soil of Europe
O God, now for Pittsburgh
my city in America
for friends I knew
the freshest blood
for the Rosenthal boys
for the other innocents
the eleven souls praying
in the synagogue
for the eleven new dead.

Jewish Eyes

burst like stars
stare back into the ghetto night
smoke and flame rage to blot them
but the iridescent eyes
gaze on the piles of shattered limbs
the thick red grief
and promise to remember

Liar

Years of watching, listening.
Your madman's painted mask,
Your tongue turned black with lies

about the gone-gone past
when all stood bundled by
as infants died
wrenched from pleading arms.

Only then no one spoke.

No sunbright shore beckoned.
Each hid behind
his own thick painted mask
lips strangled
into grinning lines ugly red
with guilt that no one owned.

Then they spoke.

You, they said, not me.
Them, they said, not us.

All the curling worms
beneath the blistered earth spit
out the filth & ash & still

they say not us.
Still you spread your lips
& say not me.

Your madman's painted mask has peeled.
Your tongue is black with lies.

Yad Vashem*

Here bloom green
carob trees
sweet with spring;
the righteous few
are not forgotten
in Our Garden.
Silence pours
from leaf and vine.

Note the smooth
Stone shapes
amid the blossoms:
the sculpted mother's
arms around
her baby:
Tenderness,
the first remembrance
of the human artist.

Beyond the blossoms
his last remembrance,
Darkness:
the dying ashes, the
tiny flames that
burn eternal
within the concrete
and basalt.

* Yad Vashem is the name of the memorial to the victims of the Holocaust in Jerusalem.

Why a Stick
based on "Woman With Stick" by Mary Ellen Raneri

I stand before you in full glory of myself.
See my proportioned torso, my sturdy limbs,
The sleekness of my skin.
My body grew full, well-nourished, beautifully shaped.
I would say perfect.
I flowered in tender, sheltered light.
I was loved. I was protected.
But it was as though I slept: much was kept from me.
Later, grown, I stepped out of my blessed sanctuary,
Awakened into a landscape split by want and rage and loathing,
Suffering of innocents without mercy or explanation.
Shocked, cowering, I wished to be other than myself:
A rock, a hill, a river, an island in the sea.
But I thought this could not be.
My flesh rebelled, turned red with fury,
I dwelt in fear for many seasons .
Only under a sturdy elm I found a measure of peace.
The leaves of this majestic tree rustled with a message:
You are not the only creature I have offered succor.
Here is my limb, I give it to you. Take it! Lean on it!
It is stout, it is strong, it is part of me, and I am part of everything.
Accept the tragic beautiful world as it is. Take it and walk free.

Acknowledgements

An Adventure (version), *Third Wednesday*, 2014
Ah, Faith, *Poetry Super Highway*, 2018
April, *Pittsburgh Post-Gazette*, 2016
Art Deco, *Philadelphia Poets*, 2018
Attention Amazon: Pittsburgh, *Pittsburgh Post-Gazette*, 2017
A Brother Writes His Blessings, *The Pittsburgh Poetry Review*, 2015
Buy A Ticket, *Pittsburgh Post-Gazette*, 2019
Carousel, Helen https://youtu.be/pLFTXuoE3Gs
Carousel, *Lummox Press*, 2017
A Climate for Children—Orange Fire, *Main Street Rag*, 2012 (version)
Collateral Circulation, *Blue Unicorn*, 2017
Counting, *Blue Unicorn*, 2020
Desperadoes, *Rockhurst Review*, 2015
Dilemma, *Pittsburgh Post-Gazette*, 2018
A Dream of My Cousin, *U.S. 1 Worksheets*, 2020
Feed Lots, *Blue Unicorn*, 2020/Pushcart Nomination
gloss and chaos, *Uppagus*, 2016
If This Was A Movie, *California Quarterly*, 2015
Lazlo's Trip, *Uppagus*, 2017
Now The Sadness, *California Quarterly*
Picnic at Belarus, Jewish Literary Journal, 2019
Questions, www.poetryxhunger.com, 2020
Spring Fever, *Pittsburgh Poetry Houses*, Randyland, 2016
This Pittsburgh Moment, 2015, *Main Street Rag*, 2016
Tikkun Olam, *Lilipoh*, 2014
Urbanity, The Writers Place, poetry competition winner, 2012- 2013

The author wishes to thank Julie Albright for her advice and careful formatting of *Buy a Ticket*.

Cover art by Judith R. Robinson

Judith R. Robinson is an editor, teacher, fiction writer, poet and visual artist. She is a 1980 summa cum laude graduate of the University of Pittsburgh. She has published 100+ poems, five poetry collections, one fiction collection, and one novel, and edited or co-edited eleven poetry collections. Her last painting exhibit was in September 2021, at the Square Café in Pittsburgh. She conducts poetry classes for Osher Lifelong Learning Institutes at Carnegie Mellon University.

Made in the USA
Monee, IL
15 February 2022

90653869R00062